DOVER · THRIFT · EDITIONS

PATRIOTISM

Quotations from Around the World

Edited by
HERB GALEWITZ

DOVER PUBLICATIONS, INC.
Mineola, New York

DOVER THRIFT EDITIONS

GENERAL EDITOR: PAUL NEGRI

EDITOR OF THIS VOLUME: THOMAS CRAWFORD

Copyright

Bibliographical Note

Patriotism: Quotations from Around the World is a new work, first published by Dover Publications, Inc., in 2003.

Library of Congress Cataloging-in-Publication Data

Patriotism : quotations from around the world / edited by Herb Galewitz.
      p. cm. (Dover Thrift Editions)
  Includes bibliographical references.
  ISBN 0-486-42690-4 (pbk.)
    1. Patriotism—Quotations, maxims, etc. I. Galewitz, Herb.

PN6084.P4P38 2003
323.6'5—dc21

2002041577

Manufactured in the United States of America
Dover Publications, Inc., 31 East 2nd Street, Mineola, N.Y. 11501

Note

FEW are neutral about patriotism; it is a topic that evokes strong feelings on all sides. Moreover, patriotism is a difficult concept to pin down. As William Inge put it, "Patriotism varies from a noble devotion to moral lunacy." In this comprehensive collection, you'll find more than 400 examples of the varied range of patriotic sentiments spanning 2,000 years—from the *amor pro patria* of ancient Rome to the moral outrage over domestic terrorism expressed by President Bill Clinton.

Included here are the utterances of patriots of all stripes: at one extreme, the ardent nationalists who believe there is no greater love than love of one's country; at the other, those who regard patriotism as a narrow and unjustified exercise in national one-upmanship, the province of those referred to in Dr. Johnson's celebrated remark: "Patriotism is the last refuge of a scoundrel."

Within these parameters lie the "My country, right or wrong" sentiments of Stephen Decatur and Theodore Roosevelt; the cynicism of H. L. Mencken ("Whenever you hear a man speak of his love of his country it is a sign that he expects to be paid for it"); the forthright utilitarianism of John Milton ("Our country is wherever we are well off"); and George Bernard Shaw's provocative proclamation that "You'll never have a quiet world till you knock the patriotism out of the human race."

These and many more comments, remarks, lyrics, quips and heartfelt observations about patriotism are contained in this thought-provoking treasury—all arranged alphabetically by author—the perfect resource for students, teachers, statesmen, public speakers—anyone interested in this absorbing and controversial topic.

Patriotism in the female sex is the most disinterested of all virtues . . . Deprived of a voice in legislation, obliged to submit to those laws which are imposed on us, is it not sufficient to make us indifferent to the public welfare? Yet all history and every age exhibit instances of patriotic virtue in the female sex; which considering our situation equals the most heroic of yours.

ABIGAIL ADAMS

Swim or sink, live or die, survive or perish with my country was my unalterable determination.

If national pride is ever justifiable or excusable, is when it springs, not from power or riches, grandeur or glory, but from a conviction of national innocence, information, and benevolence.

JOHN ADAMS

And say not thou "My country right or wrong,"
Nor shed thy blood for an unhallowed cause.

JOHN QUINCY ADAMS

If I have a wish dearer to my soul than that my ashes may be mingled with those of a Warren and a Montgomery, it is, that these American States will never cease to be free and independent.

The existence of such a government as ours, for any length of time, is a full proof of the general dissemination of knowledge and virtue throughout the whole body of the people. What object more pleasing than this can be presented to the human mind?

SAMUEL ADAMS

What pity is it
That we can die but once to serve our country.

JOSEPH ADDISON

Love of country is like love of woman—he loves her best who seeks
to bestow on her the highest good.

FELIX ADLER

Patriotism is a lively sense of collective responsibility. Nationalism
is a silly cock crowing on its own dunghill.

RICHARD ALDINGTON

A wise man's country is the world.

ARISTIPPUS

The country of every man is that one where he lives best.

ARISTOPHANES

The notion of a farseeing and despotic statesman, who can lay
down plans for ages yet unborn, is a fancy generated by the pride of
the human intellect to which facts give no support.

WALTER BAGEHOT

True patriots we; for be it understood,
We left our country for our country's good.

GEORGE BARRINGTON

But whether on the scaffold high
  Or in the battle's van,
The fittest place where man can die
  Is where he dies for man!

MICHAEL J. BARRY

O beautiful for patriot dream
  That sees beyond the years
Thine alabaster cities gleam
  Undimmed by human tears!

KATHARINE LEE BATES

America—half-brother of the world!—with something good and bad of every land.

PHILIP BAYLEY

In time of war the loudest patriots are the greatest profiteers.

AUGUST BEBEL

What is subversive today will almost certainly be patriotic tomorrow.

LUCIUS BEEBE

So strange is the transforming power of patriotic ardor that men shall almost covet disfigurement; and buoyant children shall pause in their noisy games, and with loving reverence honor those whose hands can work no more, and whose feet are no longer able to march . . .

HENRY WARD BEECHER

I pledge allegiance to my flag and the republic for which it stands: one nation, indivisible, with liberty and justice for all.

FRANCIS BELLAMY

The most valorous and morally valuable war work is that of working with impossible people.

ARNOLD BENNETT

Today the horizons flame with war. It is no time for partisanship, say men. Aye! it is the hour for the supremest partisanship—it is the hour for the partisanship of patriotism.

ALBERT J. BEVERIDGE

Patriot, n. One to whom the interests of a part seem superior to those of the whole. The dupe of statesmen and the tool of conquerors.

Patriotism, n. Combustible rubbish ready to the torch of anyone ambitious to illuminate his name.

In Dr. Johnson's famous dictionary patriotism is defined as the last resort of a scoundrel. With all due respect . . . I beg to submit that it is the first.

Un-American, adj. Wicked, intolerable, heathenish.

Diplomacy, n. The patriotic art of lying for one's country.

AMBROSE BIERCE

Not by speeches and decisions of majorities will the greatest problems of the time be decided . . . but by iron and blood.

OTTO VON BISMARCK

My patriotism stops short of my stomach.

OTTO VON BISMARCK
(on being offered a glass of German champagne)

Loyalty must arise spontaneously from the hearts of people who love their country and respect their government.

HUGO L. BLACK

There is no "Republican," no "Democrat," on the Fourth of July— all are Americans. All feel that their country is greater than party.

JAMES GILLESPIE BLAINE

Patriotism must be founded on great principles and supported by great virtue.

HENRY ST. JOHN, VISCOUNT BOLINGBROKE

I reject, I utterly reject, I denounce, as subversive of everything which we Americans hold sacred, the theory that in fighting Communism and Fascism, you must surrender Americanism.

WILLIAM E. BORAH

Next to the love of God, the love of country is the best preventive of crime. He who is proud of his country will be particularly cautious not to do anything which is calculated to disgrace it.

GEORGE BORROW

America for all its fits and starts of memory, never quite forgets those who hold the country to its grandest, most encompassing possibilities.

RANDOLPH BOURNE

No man can be a patriot on an empty stomach.

W. C. BRANN

Patriotism is a mighty precious thing when it costs nothing, but the mass of mankind consider it a very foolish thing when it curtails their self-indulgence.

JOHN BROCKENBROUGH

Patriotism takes the place of religion in France. In the service of *la patrie* the doing of one's duty is elevated into the sphere of exalted emotion.

W. C. BROWNELL

Under a despotic government there is no such thing as patriotic feeling, and its place is supplied in other ways, by private interest, public fame, and devotion to one's chief.

LA BRUYÈRE

Ah, never shall the land forget
    How gushed the life-blood of her brave,
Gushed, warm with hope and valor yet,
    Upon the soil they fought to save!

WILLIAM CULLEN BRYANT

The Beautiful, the Sacred—
Which, in all climes, men that have hearts adore
By the great title of their mother country!

E. G. BULWER-LYTTON

Off with your hat as the flag goes by!
  And let the heart have its say
You're man enough for a tear in your eye
  That you will not wipe away.

H. C. BUNNER

In general, despite all the talk about freedom, peoples and governments demand unlimited state power internally.

JAKOB BURCKHARDT

So to be patriots as not to forget that we are gentlemen.

To make us love our country, our country ought to be lovely.

EDMUND BURKE

Lay the proud usurpers low!
Tyrants fall in every foe;
Liberty's in every blow!
Forward! Let us do or die!

Wherever I wander, wherever I rove,
The hills of the Highland forever I love!

ROBERT BURNS

Were we sincere in our allegiance to the Confederate States? Yes. Does this affect our loyalty to the government of the United States? Not at all. Loyalty, free and honest loyalty to the government as it is, is not repugnant to a past loyalty to that adolescent nation whose star shone with abnormal brilliancy for a few short years, and then vanished into the blackness of eternal night.

CHARLES M. BUSBEE

We are bound by ideals that move us beyond our backgrounds, lift us above our interests and teach us what it means to be citizens. Every child must be taught these principles. Every citizen must uphold them.

GEORGE W. BUSH

Though I love my country, I do not love my countrymen.

Yes—one —the first—the last—the best—
The Cincinnatus of the West,
  Whom envy dare not hate,
Bequeath, the name of Washington
To make men blush there was but one!

He who loves not his country, can love nothing.

For what were all these country patriots born?
To hunt, and vote, and raise the price of corn?

GEORGE GORDON, LORD BYRON

The religion of Hell is patriotism and the government is an enlightened democracy.

JAMES BRANCH CABELL

Protection and patriotism are reciprocal.

JOHN C. CALHOUN

The patriot's blood's the seed of Freedom's tree.

THOMAS CAMPBELL

I should like to be able to love my country and to love justice.

ALBERT CAMUS

A steady patriot of the world alone,
The friend of every country but his own.

GEORGE CANNING

My rackets are run on strictly American lines and they're going to stay that way!

AL CAPONE

Surely the hero whose name is splashed in headlines for some singular spectacular deed of valor is no more a patriot than the unknown, steadfast citizen who year after year quietly and unselfishly benefits his nation.

ALBERT CARR

Our history is one of a people diverse in backgrounds but united in common values, facing one serious challenge after another. We have faced depressions, wars, injustice, and prevailed each time. We will prevail again, and with your help, meet fully the challenges of our time.

JIMMY CARTER

I realize that patriotism is not enough. I must have no hatred or bitterness towards anyone.

EDITH CAVELL

Let not Avarice quench the fire,
That Patriotism should inspire;
With general voice exclaim: "Away
All sordid thoughts of greater pay."

Chambers' Journal

The tumultuous love of the populace must be seized and enjoyed in its first transports . . . it will not keep.

Earl of Chesterfield

"My country right or wrong," is a thing no patriot would think of saying except in a desperate case. It is like saying, "My mother, drunk or sober!"

G. K. Chesterton

We join ourselves to no party that does not carry the flag and keep step to the music of the Union.

Rufus Choate

Nothing is sweeter than one's own country.

St. John Chrysostom

Who loves his country cannot hate mankind.

Charles Churchill

Bearing ourselves humbly before God, but conscious that we serve an unfolding purpose, we are ready to defend our native land.

Let us therefore brace ourselves to our duties, and so bear ourselves that, if the British Empire and its Commonwealth last for a thousand years, men will say, "This was their finest hour."

The gratitude of every home in our island . . . goes out to the British airmen, who undaunted by odds, unwearied in their constant challenge and mortal danger, are turning the tide of world war . . . Never in the field of human conflict was so much owed by so many to so few.

We shall defend every village, every town and every city . . . we would rather see London laid in ruins and ashes than that it should be tamely and abjectly enslaved.

In that supreme emergency we shall not hesitate to take every step, even the most drastic, to call forth from our people the last ounce and the last inch of effort of which they are capable.

I have nothing to offer but blood, toil, tears and sweat. You ask what is our policy? I will say it is to wage war—by sea, land and air, with all our might and with all the strength that God can give us; to wage war against a monstrous tyranny never surpassed in the dark lamentable catalogue of human crimes.

We shall fight in France, we shall fight on the seas and oceans, we shall fight with growing confidence and growing strength in the air. We shall fight on the beaches, we shall fight on the landing grounds, we shall fight in the fields, and in the streets, we shall fight in the hills. We shall never surrender.

WINSTON CHURCHILL

Dear are our parents, dear our children, our relatives, and our associates, but all our affections for all these are embraced in our affection for our native land.

CICERO

It is muddleheaded to say, I am in favor of this kind of political regime rather than that: what one really means is, I prefer this kind of police.

E. MICHEL CIORAN

I have heard something said about allegiance to the South: I know no South, no North, no East, no West, to which I owe any allegiance.

HENRY CLAY

How dare you suggest that we in the freest nation on earth live in tyranny? How dare you call yourselves patriots and heroes? . . . there is nothing patriotic about hating your country, or pretending that you love your country but despise your government.

BILL CLINTON

I'm a Yankee Doodle Dandy,
A Yankee Doodle do or die;
A real live nephew of my Uncle Sam's,
Born on the Fourth of July.

Many a bum show has been saved by the flag.

GEORGE M. COHAN

I, for one, do not call the sod under my feet my country. But language, religion, laws, government, blood—identity of these makes men of one country.

S. T. COLERIDGE

Proudly floats the starry banner,
  Monmouth's glorious field is won,
And in triumph Irish Molly
  Stands beside her smoking gun.

WILLIAM COLLINS

Patriotism is easy to understand in America. It means looking out for yourself by looking out for your country.

CALVIN COOLIDGE

Treason is in the air around us everywhere. It goes by the name of patriotism.

If I were a Mexican I would tell you, "Have you not room enough in your own country to bury your dead? If you come into mine, we will greet you with bloody hands, and welcome you to hospitable graves."

THOMAS CORWIN

Patriotism, to be truly American, begins with the human allegiance.

NORMAN COUSINS

Patriots are grown too shrewd to be sincere,
And we too wise to trust them.

WILLIAM COWPER

Patriotism is the vital condition of national permanence.

G. W. CURTIS

The American Flag
Here's to the red of it,
There's not a thread of it,
No, not a shred of it,
In all the spread of it,
  From foot to head,
But heroes bled for it,
Faced steel and lead for it . . .
Precious blood shed for it,
  Bathing in Red.

JOHN DALY

The tocsin we shall sound is not the alarm signal of danger: it orders the charge on the enemies of France. To conquer we have to dare, to dare again, always to dare! And France will be saved!

What! you have a whole nation as a lever, its reason as your fulcrum, and you have not yet upturned the world!

GEORGES JACQUES DANTON

Our country! In her intercourse with foreign nations may she always be in the right; but our country, right or wrong.

STEPHEN DECATUR

Patriotism is when love of your own people comes first; nationalism, when hate for people other than your own comes first.

CHARLES DE GAULLE

Patriotism is a kind of religion; it is the egg from which wars are hatched.

GUY DE MAUPASSANT

May the British Lion have his talons eradicated by the noble bill of the American Eagle, and be taught to play upon the Irish Harp and the Scotch Fiddle that music which is breathed by every empty shell that lies upon the shore of green Columbia.

CHARLES DICKENS

> Come join hand in hand brave Americans all,
> And rouse your bold hearts at fair Liberty's call;
> No tyrannous acts shall suppress your claim,
> Or stain with dishonour America's name.

JOHN DICKINSON

Patriotism depends as much on mutual suffering as on mutual success.

BENJAMIN DISRAELI

You can't prove you're an American by waving Old Glory.

HELEN GAHAGAN DOUGLAS

> And they who for their country die
> Shall fill an honored grave,
> For glory lights the soldier's tomb,
> And beauty weeps the brave.

J. R. DRAKE

Never was a patriot yet, but was a fool.

A Patriot's all-atoning name.

> Patriots in peace, assert the people's right;
> With noble stubbornness resisting might.

JOHN DRYDEN

"The American nation in the Sixth Ward is a fine people," he says. "They love th' eagle," he says, "on the back iv a dollar."

FINLEY PETER DUNNE

Nationalism is an infantile disease. It is the measles of mankind.

ALBERT EINSTEIN

Patriotism means equipped forces and a prepared citizenry.

America did not become great through softness and self-indulgence.

Of all the nations of today the future will say that there were two kinds: those that were intelligent, courageous, decisive and tireless in their support of high principle—and those that disappeared from the the earth. The true patriots of today are those who are giving their best to assure that our own country will always be found in the first of these two categories.

DWIGHT D. EISENHOWER

The white officers . . . and the black rank and file volunteered when disaster clouded the Union cause . . . Together they gave to the nation and the world undying proof that Americans of African descent possess the pride, courage, and devotion of the patriot soldier.

CHARLES WILLIAM ELIOT

I am come amongst you at this time, not as for my recreation or sport, but being resolved, in the midst and heat of the battle, to live or die amongst you all; to lay down for my God, and for my kingdom and for my people, my honor and my blood, even the dust.

QUEEN ELIZABETH I

True patriotism doesn't exclude an understanding of the patriotism of others.

QUEEN ELIZABETH II

Any relation to the land, the habit of tilling it, or mining it, or even hunting on it, generates the feeling of patriotism.

> By the rude bridge that arched the flood,
>   Their flag to April's breeze unfurled,
> Here once the embattled farmers stood,
>   And fired the shot heard 'round the world.

When a whole nation is roaring Patriotism at the top of its voice, I am fain to explore the cleanliness of its hands and the purity of its heart.

RALPH WALDO EMERSON

A man who does not wish to have his epitaph written until his country is liberated will not leave a weapon in the power of envy, or a pretense to impeach the probity which he means to preserve, even in the grave to which tyranny consigns him.

ROBERT EMMET

> Then I wish I was in Dixie,
>   Hooray! Hooray!
> In Dixie land I'll take my stand
> To live and die in Dixie.

DANIEL D. EMMETT

. . . it is the cradle and the refuge of free principles, though often persecuted, the school of religious liberty, the more precious for the struggles for which it has passed; the tombs of those who have reflected honor upon all who speak the English language; the birthplace of our fathers; the home of the Pilgrims—it is these which I venerate in England.

In hard, doubtful, unprosperous, and dangerous times, the disinterested and patriotic find their way, by a species of public instinct, unopposed, joyfully welcomed to the control of affairs.

God bless the Union; it is dearer to us for the blood of brave men which has been shed in its defence . . . Seminary Ridge, the Peach Orchard, Cemetery, Culp, and Wolf Hill, Round Top, Little Round Top, humble names, henceforward dear and famous—no lapse of time, no distance of space, shall cause you to be forgotten.

EDWARD EVERETT

Patriotism has its roots deep in the instincts and the affections. Love of country is the expansion of filial love.

D. D. FIELD

I once heard an Irishman say, "Every man loves his native land whether he was born there or not."

THOMAS FITCH

The genius of America has been its incredible ability to improve the lives of its citizens through a unique combination of governmental and free citizen activity.

I look forward to the status of private citizen with gladness and gratitude. To me, being a citizen of the United States of America is the greatest honor and privilege in the world.

GERALD R. FORD

If you find something of merit on this side of the water, you are suspected of flag-waving; if you find anything wrong, you are asked to go back where you came from.

ROBERT FORSYTHE

Conquest gives no right to the conqueror to be a tyrant; and it is no violation of right to abolish the authority which is misused.

CHARLES JAMES FOX

How beautiful is the soul of France, which since centuries past has taught right and justice to Europe and to the world! France is again the land of golden reason and benevolent thoughts, the soil of equitable magistrature, the country of Turgot, of Montesquieu, of Voltaire, of Malesherbes. Zola has merited well of his country in not despairing of justice.

ANATOLE FRANCE

Thus I consent, sir, to this Constitution because I expect no better, and because I am not sure that it is not the best. The opinions I have had of its errors, I sacrifice to the public good.

BENJAMIN FRANKLIN

Patriots need no ancestors.

FRENCH PROVERB

Liberté, égalité, fraternité

WATCHWORD OF THE FRENCH REVOLUTION

Love for one's country which is not a part of one's love for humanity is not love, but idolatrous worship.

ERICH FROMM

Originality and initiative are what I ask for my country.

ROBERT FROST

For us, patriotism is the same as the love of humanity.

MOHANDAS GANDHI

Our country is the world—our countrymen are all mankind.

WILLIAM LLOYD GARRISON

> Yet why should learning hope success at Court?
> Why should our patriots virtue's cause support?
> Why to true merit should they have regard?
> They know that virtue is its own reward.

JOHN GAY

> Fly, swift winged Fame, the news proclaim.
> From shore to shore let cannons roar,
> And joyful voices shout Columbia's name.
> Shout! Columbia's name.

DANIEL GEORGE

What is our task? To make Britain a fit country for heroes to live in.

The stern hand of fate has scourged us to an elevation where we can see the great everlasting things that matter for a nation; the great peaks of honour we had forgotten—duty and patriotism, clad in glittering white; the great pinnacle of sacrifice pointing like a rugged finger to heaven.

DAVID LLOYD GEORGE

But while the despoiled tombs of the Pharaohs mock the vanity that reared them, the name of the Hebrew who, revolting from their tyranny, strove for the elevation of his fellow men is yet a beacon light to the world.

How can a man be said to have a country when he has no right to a square inch of it?

HENRY GEORGE

Unluckily the peoples of earth do not like the smell of any but their own nationals.

Patriotism is a subject on which we must all make up our minds, an intimate matter, like love and immortality, concerning which, for our own peace and inner equilibrium, we must know where we stand.

KATHARINE FULLERTON GEROULD

When Johnny comes marching home again
    Hurrah! Hurrah!
We'll give him a hearty welcome then,
    Hurrah! Hurrah!
The men will cheer, the boys will shout,
The ladies they will all turn out,
And we'll all feel gay when Johnny comes
    marching home.

PATRICK S. GILMORE

Lawgivers or revolutionaries who promise equality and liberty at the same time are either utopian dreamers or charlatans.

The patriotism of antiquity . . . developed naturally from the whole condition of a people, its youth, its situation, its culture—with us it is an awkward imitation. Our life demands, not separation from other nations, but constant intercourse.

JOHANN WOLFGANG VON GOETHE

Such is the patriot's boast, where'er we roam,
His first, best country ever is, at home.

OLIVER GOLDSMITH

Our great modern Republic. May those who seek the blessings of
its institutions and the protection of its flag remember the obligations
they impose.

U. S. GRANT

A nation is not a heap of sand grains. It is an organism all alive, in
which each cell and germ feeds each other, and by each other is
fed . . . so does every child of America belong to America, and
America belongs to every child of hers.

You belong to your country as you belong to your mother.

EDWARD EVERETT HALE

I only regret that I have but one life to lose for my country.

NATHAN HALE

They love their land because it is their own,
And scorn to give aught other reasons why.

Strike—till the last armed foe expires;
Strike—for your altars and your fires;
Strike—for the green graves of your sires;
    God—and your native land.

FITZ-GREENE HALLECK

When you have divided and balanced the departments of government; when you have strongly connected the virtue of your rulers with their interests; when, in short, you have rendered your system as perfect as human forms can be, you must place confidence; and you must give power.

ALEXANDER HAMILTON

The loss of liberty to a generous mind is worse than death; and yet we know there have been those in all ages who, for the sake of preferment or some imaginary honor, have freely lent a helping hand to oppress, nay, to destroy, their country.

ANDREW HAMILTON

Soldiers, there is nothing left us in any quarter but what we can vindicate with our swords! . . . There is no alternative but victory or death; and if it must be death, who would not rather encounter it in battle than in flight?

HANNIBAL

You may call a man a liar, a reactionary and a racketeer and make him angry, but he will turn on you with embittered violence if you say he is not a patriot.

HARRY HANSEN

In the great fulfillment we must have a citizenship less concerned about what the government can do for it and more anxious about what it can do for the nation.

America's present need is not heroics; not nostrums but normalcy; not revolution but restoration; not surgery but serenity.

Stabilize America first, prosper America first, think of America first, exalt America first.

WARREN G. HARDING

To be radical is, in the best and only decent sense of the word, patriotic.

MICHAEL HARRINGTON

I think there is one higher office than president and I would call that patriot.

GARY HART

He serves his party best who serves the country best.

RUTHERFORD B. HAYES

A politician will do anything to keep his job—even become a patriot.

WILLIAM RANDOLPH HEARST

They wrote in the old days that it is sweet and fitting to die for one's country. But in modern war there is nothing sweet nor fitting in your dying. You will die like a dog for no good reason.

ERNEST HEMINGWAY

Caesar had his Brutus—Charles I his Cromwell—and George III may profit by their example. If this be treason, make the most of it.

Is life so dear, or peace so sweet, as to be purchased at the price of chains and slavery? Forbid it, Almighty God! I know not what course others may take; but as for me, give me liberty or give me death.

I am not a Virginian but an American.

PATRICK HENRY

The crusade is usually advertised by the middle-aged with paunches, who, after the call has been issued, leave it to the more shapely youth to gird on the breastplate of righteousness and the gas masks.

HUBERT HERRING

(The American flag.) Beautiful as a flower to those who love it, terrible as a meteor to those who hate it, it is the symbol of the power and glory, and the honor, of . . . Americans.

GEORGE FRISBE HOAR

No matter how noble the objectives of a government, if it blurs decency and kindness, cheapens human life, and breeds ill will and suspicion—it is an evil government.

ERIC HOFFER

One Flag, one Land, one Heart, one Hand,
One Nation evermore.

OLIVER WENDELL HOLMES

A glorious death is his who for his country falls.

HOMER

I don't set up for being a cosmopolite, which to my mind signifies being polite to every country except your own.

SAMP;
THOMAS HOOD

If I have to lay an egg for my country, I'll do it.

BOB HOPE

It is sweet and glorious to die for one's country.

The smoke from our native land is brighter than fire in a foreign country.

HORACE

Behold the majestic figure of Washington, whose presence must ever inspire patriotic emotions, and command the admiration and love of every American heart . . . *Maintain the Missouri Compromise!* Stir not up agitation! Give us peace!

SAM HOUSTON

It seems like th' less a statesman amounts to th' more he loves the flag.

KIN HUBBARD

You cannot be saved by valor and devotion to your ancestors. To each generation comes its patriotic duty, and upon your willingness to sacrifice and endure, as those before you have sacrificed and endured, rests the national hope.

CHARLES EVANS HUGHES

There is no such thing as a little country. The greatness of a people is no more determined by their number than the greatness of a man is determined by his height.

VICTOR HUGO

What we need are critical lovers of America—patriots who express their faith in their country by working to improve it.

HUBERT HUMPHREY

We don't want to fight,
    But, by Jingo, if we do,
We've got the ships, we've got the men,
    We've got the money, too.

G. W. HUNT

One of the great attractions of patriotism—it fulfills our worst wishes. In the person of our nation we are able, vicariously, to bully and cheat, what's more, with a feeling that we are profoundly virtuous.

ALDOUS HUXLEY

Patriotism varies from a noble devotion to a moral lunacy.

A nation is a society united by a delusion about its ancestry and by a common hatred of its neighbors.

WILLIAM R. INGE

He loves his country best who strives to make it best.

ROBERT G. INGERSOLL

Our federal Union, it must be preserved.

ANDREW JACKSON

Patriotism is a centrifugal emotion intensifying at the outskirts.

ALICE JAMES

I think patriotism is like charity—it begins at home.

HENRY JAMES

I would go to hell for my country.

But would the honest patriot, in the full tide of successful experiment, abandon a government which has so far kept us free and firm, on the theoretic and visionary fear that this government, the world's best hope, may by possibility want energy to preserve itself?

Indeed I tremble for my country when I reflect that God is just.

My affections are first for my own country, and then, generally, for all mankind.

The tree of liberty must be refreshed from time to time with the blood of patriots and tyrants. It is its natural manure.

THOMAS JEFFERSON

Our supple tribes repress their patriot throats,
And ask no questions but the price of votes.

Patriotism is the last refuge of a scoundrel.

That man is little to be envied whose patriotism would not gain force upon the plain of Marathon . . .

SAMUEL JOHNSON

Country is dear, but liberty is dearer still.

JUVENAL

I look upon the whole world as my fatherland. I look upon true patriotism as the brotherhood of man and the service of all to all.

HELEN KELLER

Let every nation know, whether it wishes us well or ill, that we shall pay any price, bear any burden, meet any hardship, support any friend, oppose any foe, in order to assure the survival and success of liberty.

And so, my fellow Americans, ask not what your country can do for you, ask what you can do for your country.

JOHN F. KENNEDY

O say does that Star Spangled Banner yet wave
O'er the land of the free and the home of the brave?

FRANCIS SCOTT KEY

Among really small nations, patriotism has a tendency to become a disease, and for lack of genuine heroes, the natives will worship brigands, thieves, and even fabulous animals.

ALEXANDER KING

Our hearts where they rocked our cradle,
   Our love where we spent our toil,
And our faith, and our hope, and our honor,
   We pledge to our native soil.

God gave all men all earth to love,
   But since our hearts are small,
Ordained for each one spot should prove
   Beloved over all.

RUDYARD KIPLING

My beloved native land! thy very sufferings make thee but dearer to my heart; thy bleeding image dwells with me when I wake, as it rests with me in the short moments of my restless sleep . . . It will accompany me when I go back to fight over again the battle of thy freedom once more.

Others spoke—you acted; and I was free! You acted and at this act of yours, tyrants trembled! humanity shouted out with joy; the downtrodden people of Magyars—the downtrodden, but not broken—raised their heads with resolution and with hope, and the brilliancy of your Stars was greeted by Europe's oppressed nations as the morning star of rising liberty.

LOUIS KOSSUTH

The mode of government is incomparably more important for a nation than the form of state.

WALTER SAVAGE LANDOR

Give me your tired, your poor,
Your huddled masses yearning to breathe free,
The wretched refuse of your teeming shore,
Send these, the homeless, tempest-tossed to me:
I lift my lamp beside the golden door.

EMMA LAZARUS

Charles Dickens shared with all his race that peculiar and almost insulting insular smugness which deplores the sins of other nations, forgetting the recentness of their own conversion.

STEPHEN LEACOCK

Burning stakes do not lighten the darkness.

STANISLAUS J. LEC

Patriotism is . . . to most men, a moral necessity. It meets and satisfies that desire for a strong, disinterested enthusiasm in life which is deeply implanted in our nature.

W. E. H. LECKY

Abandon your animosities and make your sons Americans!

ROBERT E. LEE

In Russia we must now set about building a proletarian socialist state. Long live the world socialist revolution!

VLADIMIR ILYICH LENIN

Patriotism is nothing more than a feeling of welfare, and the dread of seeing it disturbed.

STANISLAUS LESZCYNSKI

Is America a great country or what? Every day that I've been on this campaign honestly tells me the answer is "Yes."

America is more than a piece of real estate. America is a series of moral principles that begin with the right to life and liberty that the Declaration says our Creator gave us.

JOSEPH LIEBERMAN

Gold is good in its place but living, brave, patriotic men are better than gold.

"A house divided against itself cannot stand." I believe that this government cannot endure permanently half slave and half free. I do not expect the Union to be dissolved—I do not expect the house to fall—but I do expect it will cease to be divided.

This country, with its institutions, belongs to the people that inhabit it. Whenever they shall grow weary of the existing government, they can exercise their constitutional right of amending it, or their revolutionary right to dismember or overthrow it.

The mystic chords of memory, stretching from every battle and patriot grave to every living heart and hearth-stone all over this broad land, will yet swell the chorus of the Union when again touched, as surely they will be, by the better angels of our nature.

. . . that we here highly resolve that these dead shall not have died in vain—that the Nation shall, under God, have a new birth of Freedom, and that government of the people, by the people, for the people shall not perish from the earth.

With malice toward none; with charity for all; with firmness in the right, as God gives us to see the right, let us strive on to finish the work we are in; to bind up the nation's wounds . . . and cherish a just and lasting peace among ourselves and with all nations.

ABRAHAM LINCOLN

Patriotism like love is a most imperfect passion.

VACHEL LINDSAY

If a man is going to be an American at all let him be so without any qualifying adjectives; and if he is going to be something else, let him drop the word American from his personal description.

Let every man honor and love the land of his birth and the race from which he springs and keep their memory green. It is a pious and honorable duty. But let us . . . all be Americans.

HENRY CABOT LODGE

I would rather see the United States respected than loved by other nations.

HENRY CABOT LODGE, JR.

So through the night rode Paul Revere;
And so through the night went his cry of alarm
To every Middlesex village and farm,
A cry of defiance, and not of fear.

HENRY WADSWORTH LONGFELLOW

And thus we see on either hand
    We name our blessings whence they've sprung;
We call our country Father Land,
    We call our language Mother Tongue.

SAMUEL LOVER

There is something magnificent in having a country to love. It is almost like what one feels for a woman. Not so tender, perhaps, but to the full as self-forgetful.

Certainly it is no shame to a man that he should be as nice about his country as about his sweetheart.

> Where'er a human spirit strives
> After a life more true and fair,
> There is the true man's birthplace grand:
> His is a world-wide fatherland!

That pernicious sentiment, "Our country, right or wrong."

JAMES RUSSELL LOWELL

Strike at every favorable opportunity. For your homes and hearths, strike! For future generations of your sons and daughters, strike! In the name of the sacred dead, strike! Let no heart be faint. Let every arm be steeled.

Have our country's flag unfurled, and in Tokyo's sun let it wave in its full glory as a symbol of hope for the oppressed and as a harbinger of victory for the right.

And like the old soldier of that ballad, I now close my military career and just fade away, an old soldier who tried to do his duty as God gave him the light to see that duty. Good-bye.

DOUGLAS MACARTHUR

> And how can a man die better
> Than facing fearful odds,
> For the ashes of his fathers
> And the temples of his gods?

THOMAS MACAULAY

A fatherland is an association on the same soil of the living and the dead, with those yet to be born.

JOSEPH DE MAISTRE

The priceless thing America has given to me has nothing to do with money or fame. Some would call it national pride. I call it the dignity of being American.

GEORGE D. MARDIKIAN

I can show the standards, the armor, and the spoils which I have in person wrested from the vanquished. I can show the scars of many wounds received in combating the enemies of Rome. These are my statues! These are my honors, to boast of; not inherited by accident, but earned by toil, by abstinence, by valor, amid clouds of dust and seas of blood.

CAIUS MARIUS

. . . in the Middle Ages . . . If a red cross was seen marked on a house people knew that its owner was doomed . . . All the houses of Europe are now marked with the mysterious red cross. History is the judge—its executioner, the proletarian.

KARL MARX

Let us ever remember that our interest is in concord, not in conflict and that our real eminence rests in the victories of peace, not those of war.

WILLIAM McKINLEY

Love your country. Your country is the land where your parents sleep, where is spoken that language in which the chosen of your heart, blushing, whispered the first word of love; it is the home that God has given you . . .

GIUSEPPE MAZZINI

Whenever you hear a man speak of his love of his country it is a sign that he expects to be paid for it.

H. L. MENCKEN

. . . a just war . . . brings out the disinterested enthusiasm of a whole people, which gives, or is prepared to give, its most precious possession, even life itself for the defense and the vindication of things that cannot be weighed, that cannot be calculated: Justice, Honor, Peace, Liberty!

CARDINAL MERCIER

Let a person have nothing to do for his country, and he will not care for it.

J. S. MILL

Stirred up with high hopes of living to be brave men and worthy patriots, dear to God, and famous to all ages.

Let not England forget her precedence of teaching nations how to live.

Our country is wherever we are well off.

JOHN MILTON

No measure of outrages shall bear down my patience. I have been, I am, I shall be, even to the tomb, the man of the public liberty, the man of the Constitution . . . woe to the privileged orders! For privileges shall have an end, but the people is eternal.

MIRABEAU

Those who give the first shock to a state are the first overwhelmed in its ruin.

MICHEL E. MONTAIGNE

The love of country produces good manners; and good manners, love of country.

MONTESQUIEU

This type of thing may be tolerated by the French, but we are British, thank God.

BERNARD MONTGOMERY

English, Scotchmen, Jews, do well in Ireland—Irishmen never; even the patriot has to leave Ireland to get a hearing.

GEORGE MOORE

There's one beneficial effect of going to Moscow. You come home waving the American flag with all your might.

MARY TYLER MOORE

Far dearer the grave or the prison,
    Illumed by one patriot name,
Than the trophies of all who have risen
    On liberty's ruins to fame!

THOMAS MOORE

The trouble with these international events is that they attract foreigners.

ROBERT MORLEY

The English, who now feel inferior to almost every nation on earth, at least have the Welsh to look down on.

JAN MORRIS

Italy, gentlemen, wants peace, wants quiet, wants work, wants calm; we will give it with love, if that be possible, or with strength, if that be necessary.

Italy! Italy! Entirely and universally Fascist! The Italy of the Black Shirt Revolution, rise to your feet, let the cry of your determination rise to the skies and reach our soldiers in East Africa.

Let all parties perish, ours along with the others, so long as our country is safe.

BENITO MUSSOLINI

Soldiers! Your country has a right to expect great things of you. Justify her expectations! . . . All, when they return home, would wish to say proudly, "I was with the victorious Army of Italy."

Who saves his country violates no law.

NAPOLEON

. . . patriotism, as I see it, is often an arbitrary veneration of real estate above principle.

GEORGE JEAN NATHAN

England expects every man will do his duty.

HORATIO NELSON

What has made America great has not been what government has done for the people, but what the people have done for themselves.

RICHARD NIXON

Oh, my friends, I will keep you clear of all treachery—there shall be no bargain, no compromise with England—we shall take nothing but repeal, and a Parliament in College Green.

The Irish were made more thirsty for liberty by the drop that fell on their parched lips.

DANIEL O'CONNELL

Nationalism means that every little group of human twerps with its own slang, haircut and pet name for God should have a country.

P. J. O'ROURKE

I must be the luckiest man in the world. Not only am I bisexual, I am also Welsh.

JOHN OSBORNE

A man's house is his castle, and whilst he is quiet, he is as well guarded as a prince in his castle. This writ, if it should be declared legal, would totally annihilate this privilege.

JAMES OTIS

Love of country is more potent than reason itself.

OVID

I believe in the United States of America as a Government of the people, by the people, for the people . . . a perfect Union one and inseparable; established upon those principles of freedom, equality, justice and humanity for which American patriots sacrificed their lives and fortunes.

WILLIAM TYLER PAGE

The world is my country, all mankind are my brethren, and to do good is my religion.

These are the times that try men's souls. The summer soldier and the sunshine patriot will, in this crisis, shrink from the service of their country; but he that stands it *now*, deserves the love and thanks of man and woman.

THOMAS PAINE

We want the energy, the patriotism, the talents, and the work of every Irishman to insure that this great experiment shall be a successful one. We want, sir, all creeds and all classes in Ireland. We cannot consent to look upon a single Irishman as not belonging to us.

CHARLES STEWART PARNELL

The triumph of demagogies is short-lived. But the ruins are eternal.

CHARLES PIERRE PÉGUY

There is no other land like thee,
　　Nor dearer shore;
Thou art the shelter of the free;
The home, the port of Liberty
Thou hast been, and shalt ever be,
　　Till Time is o'er.

JAMES GATES PERCIVAL

Does success gild crime into patriotism, and the want of it change heroic self-devotion to imprudence?

WENDELL PHILLIPS

Oh, is not this a holy spot!
　　'Tis the high place of Freedom's birth!
God of our fathers, is it not
　　The holiest spot of all the earth?

JOHN PIERPONT
(*about Bunker Hill*)

Millions for defense, but not one cent for tribute.

CHARLES C. PINCKNEY

If I were an American, as I am an Englishman, while a foreign troop was landed in my country, I never would lay down my arms! Never! never! never!

WILLIAM PITT

There can be no affinity nearer than our country.

PLATO

A patriot is a fool in ev'ry age.

> A brave man struggling in the storms of fate,
> And greatly falling, with a falling state,
> While Cato gives his little senate laws,
> What bosom beats not in his country's cause?

Who dare to love their country and be poor.

ALEXANDER POPE

Remove not the ancient landmarks which thy fathers have set up.

PROVERBS XXII. 28

We all did our duty, which, in the patriot's, soldier's, and gentleman's language, is a very comprehensive word, of great honour, meaning, and import.

RUDOLF ERICH RASPE

The success story of America is neighbor helping neighbor.

RONALD REAGAN

Let tyranny reign but one day, and on the morrow there would not remain a single patriot.

We must crush both the interior and exterior enemies of the Republic, or perish with her. And in this situation, the first maxim of your policy should be to conduct the people by reason and the enemies of the people by terror.

ROBESPIERRE

As religion is imitated and mocked by hypocrisy, so public duty is parodied by patriotism.

J. E. THOROLD ROGERS

The United States never lost a war or won a conference.

WILL ROGERS

I pledge you, I pledge myself, to a new deal for the American people. Let us all here assembled constitute ourselves prophets of a new order of competence and courage.

No matter how long it will take us to overcome this premeditated invasion, the American people, in their righteous might, will win through to absolute victory.

This great nation will endure as it has endured, will revive and will prosper. So first of all, let me assert my firm belief that the only thing we have to fear is fear itself—nameless, unreasoning, unjustified terror which paralyzes needed efforts to convert retreat into advance.

The life of a nation is the fullness and the measure of its will to win.

And with that inner strength that comes to a free people conscious of their duty, conscious of the righteousness of what they do, they will—with divine help and guidance—stand their ground against this latest assault upon their democracy, their sovereignty and their freedom.

FRANKLIN D. ROOSEVELT

A man who is good enough to shed his blood for his country is good enough to be given a square deal afterwards.

The useful member of the brotherhood of nations is that nation which is most thoroughly saturated with the national ideal.

Don't spread patriotism too thin.

The hyphenated American always hoists the American flag underneath.

There can be no fifty-fifty Americanism in this country. There is room here for only 100% Americanism, only for those who are Americans and nothing else.

I preach to you, then, my countrymen, that our country calls not for the life of ease, but for the life of strenuous endeavor.

. . . at present the man who loves other countries as much as he does his own is quite as noxious a member of society as the man who loves other women as much as he loves his wife.

A hyphenated American is not an American at all. Our allegiance must be purely to the United States. We must unsparingly condemn any man who holds any other allegiance.

THEODORE ROOSEVELT

Rally 'round the flag, boys.

GEORGE FREDERICK ROOT

> Patriots, to arms!
> Form your battalions,
> Let's march, let's march!
> May the tyrant's foul blood water our
>   furrows!

CLAUDE-JOSEPH ROUGET DE L'ISLE

As soon as any man says of the affairs of state, What does it matter to me? the state may be given up as lost.

JEAN JACQUES ROUSSEAU

It is precisely in accepting death as the end of all, and in laying down, on that sorrowful condition, his life for his friends, that the hero and patriot of all time has become the glory and safety of his country.

Nothing is permanently helpful to any race or condition of men but the spirit that is in their own hearts, kindled by the love of their native land.

JOHN RUSKIN

Patriotism is the willingness to kill and be killed for trivial reasons.

BERTRAND RUSSELL

It is sweet to serve one's country by deeds, and it is not absurd to serve her by words.

For country, children, hearth, and home.

SALLUST

To me, it seems a dreadful indignity to have a soul controlled by geography.

GEORGE SANTAYANA

The highest bliss of the human soul is love, and the noblest love is devotion to our fatherland.

FRIEDRICH VON SCHLEGEL

Our country, right or wrong. When right to be kept right; when wrong to be put right.

CARL SCHURZ

Here, soldiers, here we must make our stand! Here we must fight, as if we fought before the walls of Rome!

Let every man bear in mind that it is not only his own person, but his wife and children he must now defend! Now let the thought of them alone possess his mind!

PUBLIUS SCIPIO

Breathes there a man with soul so dead,
Who never to himself hath said,
    This is my own, my native land?

Stood for his country's glory fast,
And nailed her colours to the mast.

SIR WALTER SCOTT

Men love their country, not because it is great, but because it is their own.

SENECA

Had I a dozen sons, each in my love alike, . . . I had rather have eleven die nobly for their country, than one voluptuously surfeit out of action.

Be just and fear not; let all the ends thou aimest at, be thy country's, thy God's, and truth's.

I do love
My country's good with a respect more tender,
More holy and profound, than mine own life.

One drop of blood drawn from thy country's bosom
Should grieve thee more than streams of foreign gore.

Who is here so vile that will not love his country?

WILLIAM SHAKESPEARE

O Columbia, the gem of the ocean,
   The home of the brave and the free,
The shrine of each patriot's devotion,
   A world offers homage to thee.

DAVID T. SHAW

The national anthem belongs to the eighteenth century. In it you find us ordering God about to do our political dirty work.

What they called patriotism was a conviction that because they were born in Tooting or Camberwell, they were the natural superiors of Beethoven, of Rodin, of Ibsen, of Tolstoy and all other benighted foreigners.

. . . but you will never find an Englishman in the wrong. He does everything on principle. He fights you on patriotic principles; he robs you on business principles; he enslaves you on imperial principles.

Patriotism is your conviction that this country is superior to all other countries because you were born in it.

When a bishop at the first shot abandons the worship of Christ and rallies his flock around the altar of Mars, he may be acting patriotically . . . but that does not justify him in pretending . . . that Christ is, in effect, Mars.

You'll never have a quiet world till you knock the patriotism out of the human race.

GEORGE BERNARD SHAW

The proper means of increasing the love we bear to our native country is to reside some time in a foreign one.

WILLIAM SHENSTONE

Cease being the slave of a party and you become its deserter.

JULES SIMON

If noble death be virtue's chiefest part,
We above all men are by Fortune blest,
Striving with freedom's crown to honor Greece,
We died, and here in endless glory rest.

SIMONIDES

If it were not necessary to eat or wear clothes, Russia would be the greatest country in the world.

YAKOV SMIRNOFF

No other factor in history, not even religion, has produced so many wars as has the clash of national egotisms sanctified by the name of patriotism.

PRESERVED SMITH

My country, 'tis of thee,
Sweet land of liberty,
   Of thee I sing:
Land where our fathers died,
Land of the Pilgrim's pride,
From every mountain side
   Let freedom ring.

SAMUEL F. SMITH

True patriotism is of no party.

TOBIAS SMOLLETT

The virtue of patriotism is subordinate in most souls to individual and family aggrandizement.

ELIZABETH CADY STANTON AND SUSAN B. ANTHONY

Do not . . . regard the critics as questionable patriots. What were Washington, Jefferson and Adams but profound critics of the colonial status quo?

When an American says that he loves his country, he means not only that he loves the New England hills, the prairies glistening in the sun, the wide and rising plains, the great mountains, and the sea. He means that he loves an inner air, an inner light in which freedom lives and in which a man can draw the breath of self-respect.

It was always accounted a virtue in a man to love his country. With us it is something more than a virtue. It is a necessity.

The founding fathers did not think it was "soft" or "un-American" to respect the opinion of others, and today for a man to love his country truly, he must also know how to love mankind.

The patriots are those who love America enough to wish to see her as a model to mankind.

What do we mean by patriotism in the context of our times? . . . A patriotism that puts country ahead of self; a patriotism that is not short, frenzied outbursts of emotion, but the tranquil and steady dedication of a lifetime.

ADLAI E. STEVENSON

Patriotism knows neither latitude nor longitude. It is not climatic.

EMERY A. STORRS

> Here shall the Press the People's right maintain,
> Unaw'd by influence and unbrib'd by gain;
> Here patriot Truth her glorious precepts draw,
> Pledg'd to Religion, Liberty, and Law.

JOSEPH STORY

There is the National flag. He must be cold, indeed, who can look upon its folds rippling in the breeze without pride of country. If in a foreign land, the flag is companionship, and country itself, with all its endearments.

CHARLES SUMNER

Patriotism is a praiseworthy competition with one's ancestors.

TACITUS

> Britain's myriad voices call,
> Sons, be welded, each and all
> Into one imperial whole;
> One with Britain heart and soul,
> One fleet, one flag, one life, one throne—
> Britons hold your own!
>
> That man's the best Cosmopolite
> Who loves his native country best.

There is no glory like his who saves his country.

ALFRED, LORD TENNYSON

If you want a symbolic gesture, don't burn the flag, wash it.

NORMAN THOMAS

It is a bad witness to the goodness of a regime when people begin to praise it only after they have ceased to believe in the possibility of its restoration.

ALEXIS DE TOCQUEVILLE

From dunghills deep of blackest hue
Your dirt-bred patriots spring to view.

JOHN TRUMBULL

National enthusiasm is the great nursery of genius.

HENRY THEODORE TUCKERMAN

In the beginning of a change, the patriot is a scarce man, and brave and hated and scorned. When his cause succeeds, the timid join him, for then it costs nothing to be a patriot.

Patriotism, what a humbug it is; it is a word which always commemorates a robbery. There isn't a foot of land in the world which doesn't represent the ousting and reousting of a long line of successive owners.

MARK TWAIN

A station of perpetual safety will be awarded you, for the exertion of a trifling labor against the Turks.

POPE URBAN II (*First Crusade, 1095*)

Oh, it's home again and home again, America for me!
I want a ship that's westward bound to plough the rolling sea
To the blessed land of Room Enough beyond the ocean bars,
Where the air is full of sunlight and the flag is full of stars.

HENRY VAN DYKE

A real patriot is the fellow who gets a parking ticket and rejoices that the system works.

BILL VAUGHAN

Patriotism may be defined as a sense of partisan solidarity in respect of prestige.

THORSTEIN VEBLEN

Thus it behooves the lawmaker to prevent as much as he can the storm's disaster by wise counsel. But if under the pretext of revolution it becomes necessary, in order to be a patriot, to become the declared protector of murder and robbery—then I am a "Moderate"!

PIERRE VERGNIAUD

The noblest motive is the public good.

VIRGIL

How dear to all good hearts is their fatherland.

We must love our country, even though it treats us with injustice.

Whoever serves his country well has no need of ancestors.

VOLTAIRE

All those men [pretended patriots] have their price.

SIR ROBERT WALPOLE

I have alreddy given two cousins to the war, & I stand reddy to sacrifiss my wife's brother ruther'n not see the rebelyin krusht.

ARTEMUS WARD

A great and lasting war can never be supported on this principle (patriotism) alone. It must be aided by a prospect of interest, or some reward.

Guard against postures of pretended patriotism.

We must not, in so great a contest, expect to meet with nothing but sunshine.

The name of American, which belongs to you in your national capacity, must always exalt the just pride of patriotism more than any appellation derived from local discrimination.

GEORGE WASHINGTON

Let our object be, our country, our
whole country, and nothing but our country.

I shall know but one country. The ends I am at shall be my country's, my God's, and Truth's. I was born an American; I will live an American; I shall die an American.

Thank God! I—I also—am an American!

It is my living sentiment and, by the blessing of God, it shall be my dying sentiment—Independence now and Independence forever.

The Muse inspiring our Fathers was the Genius of Liberty, all on fire with a sense of oppression, and a resolution to throw it off. The whole world was the stage, and higher characters than princes trod it.

Liberty and union, now and forever, one and inseparable.

DANIEL WEBSTER

. . . one who dies for his cause in cooler blood is a greater hero than the one who dies intoxicated by hysteria.

DIXON WECTER

> O Canada! Our home and native land!
> True patriot love in all thy sons command.
> With glowing hearts we see thee rise,
> The True North strong and free!
> From far and wide, O Canada!
> We stand on guard for thee.
> God keep our land.

ROBERT STANLEY WEIR

The Athenian democracy suffered much from that narrowness of patriotism which is the ruin of all nations.

Patriotism has become a mere national self-assertion, a sentimentality of flag-cheering with no constructive duties.

The crazy combative patriotism that plainly threatens to destroy civilization is very largely begotten by the schoolmaster and the schoolmistress in their history lessons. They take the growing mind at a naturally barbaric phase and they inflame and fix its barbarism.

H. G. WELLS

Everybody likes to hear about a man laying down his life for his country, but nobody wants to hear about a country giving her shirt for her planet.

E. B. WHITE

"Shoot, if you must, this old gray head,
But spare your country's flag," she said.

They went where duty seemed to call,
They scarcely asked the reason why;
They only knew they could but die,
And death was not the worst of all!

JOHN GREENLEAF WHITTIER

Patriotism is the virtue of the vicious.

OSCAR WILDE

Thus I send you out there to avenge wrong and enforce reparation. I will not rest until the German flag flies victorious from the walls of Peking, flies above the Chinese, and dictates the terms of peace to the Chinese.

KAISER WILHELM II

What is good for the country is good for General Motors, and what's good for General Motors is good for the country.

CHARLES E. WILSON

America lives in the heart of every man everywhere who wishes to find a region where he will be free to work out his destiny as he chooses.

The flag is the embodiment, not of sentiment, but of history.

The lines of red [in the flag] are lines of blood, nobly and unselfishly shed by men who loved the liberty of their fellow men more than they loved their own lives and fortunes.

When I think of the flag which our ships carry . . . I see alternate strips of parchment upon which are written the rights of liberty and justice and strips of blood spilled to vindicate those rights, and then— in the corner—a prediction of the blue serene into which every nation may swim that stands for these great things.

Our whole duty, for the present at any rate, is summed up in the motto: America first . . .

WOODROW WILSON

The impossibility of a retreat makes no difference in the situation of men resolved to conquer or die; and believe me, my friends, if your conquest could be bought with the blood of your general, he would most cheerfully resign a life which he has so long devoted to his country.

GENERAL WOLFE

I am a One Hundred Percent American; I am a super patriot.

WILLIAM W. WOOLLCOTT

A patriot is a useful member of society, capable of enlarging all minds and bettering all hearts with which he comes in contact; a useful member of the human family, capable of establishing fundamental principles and of merging his own interests, those of his associates and those of his nation in the interests of the human race.

FRANCES WRIGHT

Patriotism is not, as sentimentalists like to assert, one of the profoundest of man's noblest instincts.

An honest patriot today may feel extremely virtuous, but he is none the less an anachronism wandering about a powder-magazine with a torchlight.

I. A. R. WYLIE

Considering the law of survival of ancient and modern races, if we want to save China and to preserve the Chinese race, we must certainly promote nationalism.

SUN YAT-SEN

A fatherland focuses a people.

A fig for your feuds and vendettas. Germans and Frenchmen, Irishmen and Englishmen, Jews and Russians, into the crucible with you all. God is making the American.

ISRAEL ZANGWILL